Hello, Gorgeous!

So, you've decided to dip your toes back into the dating pool, huh? Well, buckle up, because dating after 50 is like a fresh, delicious glass of sparkling lemonade—it's refreshing, zesty, and gets better with every sip. Trust me, there's a whole world of exciting possibilities out there just waiting for you to dive in. Sure, it might feel a little like stepping onto a new dance floor, but you've got the moves. You've always had the moves. Now, it's all about embracing the beat and having fun along the way.

Dating after 50 is absolutely thrilling. Why? Because you've lived a little (or a lot!) and you're now in this amazing place of self-assurance and authenticity. No more pretending to be someone you're not. You know what you like, what you don't, and most importantly, you know how to go after what you deserve. And guess what? You're deserving of all the amazing, fun, exciting connections that come your way—whether that's a passionate romance, a deep friendship, or something in between. This isn't just about finding someone else; it's about rediscovering you in the process.

So get ready to fall in love—with yourself first, and then with the possibility of what's out there. There are a lot of myths to bust, fun to have, and amazing connections to explore. Dating after 50 is not only possible, it's actually one of the best life chapters you'll write.

Busting Through Those Fake Walls About Age and Romance

Okay, let's get one thing straight right off the bat: age is just a number. If anyone tells you that you're "too old" for love, or that romance is for the young folks, well, tell them to go take a nap (they obviously need one). Dating after 50 is not about putting up with "leftover" options or settling for something that doesn't light you up. Oh no, it's about embracing your full self and attracting someone who's on the same wavelength.

Let's clear up some of the most common stereotypes about love and age.

Lie #1: It's Too Late for Me to Find Love. Really? Tell that to all the people who find true love in their 50s, 60s, or even 70s! In fact, as you get older, you actually have a clearer sense of what you want (and don't want). You're more experienced, more discerning, and more likely to recognize a good match when you see one. The best part? You're not rushing to "settle down"— you're just out there looking for connection, whatever that might look like.

Lie #2: People My Age Aren't Interested in Dating. Says who? The dating pool after 50 is full of vibrant, passionate people who are just as ready for adventure, love, and companionship as anyone else. You're not alone in this—whether it's online dating, social events, or a weekend hike, there are plenty of opportunities to meet people who share your energy and curiosity for life.

Lie #3: Romance is for the Young. What? Tell that to all the people in their 50s, 60s, and beyond who are living their best love lives! Romance is for everyone—it's just that, at this stage, it's more likely to be seasoned, thoughtful, and real. Forget the drama; we're talking about real connection, respect, and chemistry. You've got the tools to make your romantic life sizzle, no matter your age.

Lie #4: Dating After 50 is Awkward and Weird. It is? Sure, it's a little different from dating in your 20s or 30s, but that doesn't make it weird. You're more comfortable in your own skin now, and that's so attractive. You've got a better sense of humor about life, and let's be honest, that makes everything more fun. Dating after 50 is an adventure in authenticity—it's about embracing the joy of connecting with someone who gets you.

Embracing Fun, Self-Discovery, and Confidence
Here's a little secret—dating after 50 is way more fun than you might think. Gone are the days of "trying to impress" or "getting it right." At this point in your life, the key to successful dating is embracing joy, curiosity, and your true self. Think about it—no more pretending to be someone you're not. No more playing games. Instead, you're all about the adventure of discovering new people, new connections, and yes, new parts of yourself in the process.

Self-discovery doesn't stop at 50—it gets better. You're constantly evolving and finding new things that light you up. Maybe it's picking up a hobby you've always wanted to try, exploring a new city, or saying yes to that spontaneous date with someone you never thought you'd connect with. The possibilities are endless. And guess what? You've earned the confidence to explore them.

Confidence isn't about being perfect. It's about being comfortable in your own skin and knowing that you are enough, just as you are. And trust me, that confidence is magnetic. People are drawn to authenticity, so when you show up as your true self, you're already ahead of the game.

So, set the tone for your dating journey with an open mind and a playful heart. Whether you're meeting someone for coffee or going on a spontaneous road trip, embrace the excitement. Remember—this is about you, not about "getting it right." The more you embrace the adventure of self-discovery, the more fun you'll have.

The Importance of Mindset: Optimism and Openness as Keys to Success
Mindset, baby, mindset! The way you approach dating after 50 can make all the difference. If you walk into a date thinking it's going to be awkward or disappointing, chances are, that's exactly how it'll feel. But if you approach it with an open heart and mind and an optimistic attitude, you'll be amazed at what can unfold.

Optimism is your best friend in this journey. It's about believing that there's someone out there who will appreciate you for who you are. It's about staying open to new experiences and not letting past disappointments cloud your view of the future. You're not looking for perfection, just connection—and that is absolutely something worth believing in.

Let's be real: not every date will be a match made in heaven. But that's okay! Every experience is an opportunity to learn, grow, and understand more about yourself. Dating is not a race; it's an ongoing adventure. You don't have to be in a rush to find "the one" because the right people will cross your path at the right time. Keep the faith, stay positive, and watch how your mindset transforms your experience.

Openness is also crucial. Be open to different types of connections and people. Maybe you'll meet someone who doesn't check all the boxes, but sparks fly in ways you never expected. Maybe you'll find a friend who becomes your greatest companion or a casual date that turns into something meaningful. The beauty of dating after 50 is that it's all about exploration and growth, and you're never too old to experience something new.

So, here's to keeping your heart open, your mind positive, and your expectations light. The possibilities are endless, and love, laughter, and adventure are just around the corner. Ready to start? Let's go!

Chapter 1: The New Dating Landscape

Welcome to the wild, wonderful world of dating after 50, where the adventure is just getting started! Whether you're freshly single or have been on your own for a while, dating in your 50s—and beyond—has a certain magic to it. Sure, things have changed since your last round of romance (hello, flip phones and landlines), but change isn't always a bad thing. In fact, it can be downright exciting!

Gone are the days of waiting around for the phone to ring or trying to catch someone's eye across the bar. Instead, we're entering a whole new world where your perfect match could be just a swipe, click, or even a serendipitous coffee shop encounter away. The best part? You're 50-something, and you've got a lifetime of wisdom, confidence, and self-assurance that makes you way more interesting than you were in your 20s. You know exactly who you are, what you want, and, most importantly, what you don't want—and that makes all the difference.

So, let's dive into the brave new world of dating after 50, where technology and traditional meet-ups collide. Whether you're a fan of dating apps or more of a "meet me in person" type, I'll give you the lowdown on how things have changed, why the new dating landscape is nothing to fear, and how to embrace it with excitement, optimism, and maybe even a bit of that old-school charm.

The Shift from Traditional to Digital: Welcome to the 21st Century

Remember the days of meeting someone at a party? Maybe you had a mutual friend introduce you, and you'd chat over a drink or awkwardly linger by the snack table, wondering if it was time to make your move. Or maybe you'd get their number from a friend and hope they didn't write it down wrong (looking at you, sticky notes). Back then, a phone call or a few dates was all you needed to get to know someone.

But fast forward to today, and dating looks a little different. Enter the world of online dating. Instead of trying to figure out the perfect time to ask for someone's number, now we're swiping left and right—seemingly at lightning speed. The options are endless, and suddenly, meeting someone feels like choosing an outfit at a boutique: a little overwhelming but also thrilling.

Now, hold up. I get it. Maybe you're thinking, "But I'm not tech-savvy! I can barely send a text without autocorrect messing it up. How am I supposed to navigate this dating app world?" Don't worry, you're not alone. It can feel a bit like trying to learn a new language at first (Duolingo, anyone?). But trust me, once you've got the hang of it, dating apps can be a fun and easy way to meet new people. Plus, they can help you skip the awkward small talk and get right to the juicy stuff: connection!

Apps like Tinder, Bumble, and Hinge are all the rage these days, and they've even got options tailored for people over 50, so you're not competing with the 20-year-olds out there. These platforms give you a chance to present your best self—no awkward first moments to stumble through—and help you find people who are genuinely interested in the same kind of relationship you are. Think of it as shopping for your future partner in a well-curated online store.

Still, it's not all about screens. The apps may have changed the way we meet people, but the basic principles of attraction and connection? Those have stayed pretty much the same. You're still looking for someone you can share a laugh with, who shares your values (and maybe your taste in music), and who'll accept you just as you are.

Understanding Dating Apps: The Digital Playground
Okay, now let's talk about the apps themselves. There are more than a few options out there, and while it can be a bit overwhelming at first, once you know what's what, it's like riding a bike—though hopefully with a little less falling over and maybe a fancy little bell on the handlebars.

First, let's talk about Tinder—the app that's synonymous with quick dates and instant connections. While it's most famous for its casual dating vibe, there are plenty of people on Tinder looking for something real, too. If you're a fan of the "right swipe" (who isn't?) and want to see who's out there near you, it's a fast and fun way to dip your toe into the world of online dating. It's like an all-you-can-eat buffet—lots of options, and you get to choose exactly what you want.

Bumble is another favorite, and it has a little twist—the women make the first move. Yes, ladies, if you're tired of waiting for someone to message you, Bumble flips the script and lets you take charge. It's empowering, it's fun, and it could be your ticket to a meaningful connection. Plus, no more agonizing over whether or not to text someone first.

Then there's Hinge, a dating app designed for people who are looking for a little more than just a hookup. It's less about the quick swipes and more about meaningful conversations, with prompts that make it easier to break the ice. Want to show off your sense of humor or let someone know your favorite hobby? Hinge's prompts give you a way to really express who you are beyond just your photos.

Now, if you're looking for something a little more niche (no judgment here—sometimes you just want a group of people who share your passion for something specific), there are apps like OurTime and SilverSingles, which cater specifically to the over-50 crowd. These sites take away the confusion of having to weed through younger profiles and focus on connecting you with people who are more aligned with your stage of life. It's like a tailor-made suit—perfectly fitted to your needs.

The Ups and Downs of Online Dating

Okay, so what's the catch? As with anything, there are pros and cons to online dating, and it's important to know what you're getting into. Let's take a quick tour of the ups and downs of the digital dating world:

The Ups

- **Endless Options**: You've got access to a whole world of people you wouldn't normally meet. It's like being at a party where the guest list is endless—new faces, new opportunities, new party favors.
- **More Control**: No more waiting for someone to call. You're in the driver's seat, making your own decisions about who you want to talk to and when. Feel like reaching out – Just do it!

- **Convenience**: You can date on your own time—whether that's over lunch break or while you're sipping your morning coffee. This is about you and your schedule. Want to take a break? That works too!

The Downs
- **Too Many Choices**: It can be overwhelming to sift through profiles, looking for that one special connection. Sometimes, it feels like shopping for a new pair of shoes—everything looks cute, but nothing feels quite right.
- **Fake Profiles**: Ugh. It's one of the unfortunate realities of online dating. Some people aren't as honest as others. But the key is to look out for the warning signs and trust your instincts.
- **Emotional Rollercoaster**: Let's be real—online dating can be a wild ride. Some days, you might feel like you've found your soulmate. Other days, you might feel like giving up after a bad experience. But hang in there, because it's all part of the journey.

And Just Like That, You're Ready to Dive In!
Well, look at you, ready to tackle the exciting, ever-evolving world of dating after 50! The dating landscape may have changed a lot over the years, but guess what? That just means more opportunities for you to have fun, connect, and find what you're looking for. Whether you're exploring the online dating world or reconnecting with people through hobbies, travel, or mutual friends, the options are endless.

You've got a lifetime of wisdom and experience on your side, and that's what makes you a catch—no matter what age you are! You've learned how to handle the ups and downs of life, and now, you get to embrace this next chapter with a fresh, exciting perspective. Dating after 50 isn't about rushing into something or checking off boxes—it's about enjoying the journey, meeting new people, and learning more about yourself along the way.

As you step into the world of modern dating, take a deep breath, have fun, and stay open to whatever comes your way. The best part? You're in charge. You get to decide how you date, who you date, and what you want out of it.

The world is full of possibilities, and now's the time to grab them. Whether you're looking for a meaningful connection, a fun date, or just some new experiences, you're ready to dive in with confidence, enthusiasm, and an open heart. The adventure's just beginning!

Chapter 2: Dating the Old-School Way

Alright, let's take a little detour from the digital world and get back to basics. No swiping, no profiles, no emojis—just good old-fashioned face-to-face interaction. Yep, we're talking about the old-school way of dating, where you actually meet someone in person and get to know them the way people did before texting and apps became the norm. And guess what? It's still one of the best ways to find connection, chemistry, and—dare we say it—love.

Sure, the world is full of tech-savvy, swipe-happy singles, but there's something timelessly charming about the traditional way of dating. No filters. No screens. Just real, raw, and spontaneous interactions. Ready to step into a world where you make the first move with a smile and maybe—just maybe—hand over your number on a napkin?

The Magic of Real-Life Encounters: Is This the New Romance?

There's something undeniably romantic about meeting someone in real life. It's the stuff of movies, isn't it? The accidental eye contact across a crowded coffee shop. The impromptu conversation while reaching for the last bottle of wine (okay, maybe that was just us). The serendipity of crossing paths in the grocery store aisle and suddenly finding someone whose smile is as warm as the coffee in your hand.

In an era where we're often glued to screens, these authentic, offline encounters are golden. And if you're over 50 and back in the dating game, these spontaneous meet-cutes can feel like a breath of fresh air. Sure, it's easy to feel like the world is moving faster than you can keep up, but there's still magic in slow, face-to-face connections.

The beauty of meeting someone in person is that you get to feel that instant spark. Maybe it's chemistry, maybe it's the way their eyes light up when they smile, or maybe it's just how easy the conversation flows. Either way, meeting someone face-to-face adds an element of mystery and excitement that you can't get from a text message.

Let's talk about a few places where these magical moments tend to happen
- **Coffee Shops**: A classic! Whether it's a local café or the trendy spot with the cutest barista, coffee shops are a haven for casual conversations and unexpected connections. Don't be afraid to make eye contact or even start a chat about the latest bestseller or that weird latte art you've never seen before.
- **The Grocery Store**: Seriously, who knew buying oranges could be a flirtation hotspot? It's the one place where you definitely bump into someone while reaching for the same product. Whether it's discussing the merits of different kinds of pasta or helping each other pick out the best tomatoes, the grocery store is an underrated place to meet someone who just might become your next date.
- **Farmers' Markets**: Picture this: you're picking out fresh flowers, and you spot someone reaching for the same bunch of daisies. What starts as a shared appreciation for colorful blooms could easily turn into a conversation about your favorite ways to

cook with fresh herbs. Bonus points if you both end up chatting about where the best local bakery is.

- **Community Events or Classes**: Local events, such as book readings, cooking classes, or art shows, are perfect for meeting people who share your interests. You already have something in common (the event or class), so it's a natural conversation starter. And you're not just meeting someone randomly—you're meeting them in a space where you already vibe over the same things. It's a no-pressure situation, but with plenty of opportunities for connection.

Making the First Move: Confidence is Key

If you want to meet someone the old-school way, you've gotta be ready to make the first move. And I don't mean standing on the sidelines waiting for someone to notice you. I mean taking that bold step and striking up a conversation.

I know, I know—it can feel intimidating. But remember, you're not a teenager anymore. You've lived a full life. You've got wisdom, charm, and a sense of self that people will notice. Plus, confidence is magnetic. If you walk into a room, smiling, standing tall, and radiating positive energy, people will be drawn to you like a moth to a flame.

Here's how to make the first move without feeling awkward or cheesy

- **Smile**: Start with a warm, genuine smile. It's the easiest way to communicate that you're friendly and open to a conversation. And let's be real—everyone loves a smile.

- **Make Eye Contact**: This is the key to non-verbal communication. If you catch someone's eye across the room, hold the gaze for a moment longer than usual. If they smile back or look away shyly, that's your cue. Now, you're not just hoping for an interaction—you're creating one.
- **The Compliment**: A simple, sincere compliment can go a long way. "I love your jacket—where did you get it?" or "You have such a great energy about you" are both great icebreakers. The key here is to make it feel natural and genuine, not forced.
- **Start with a Question**: People love to talk about themselves, so why not give them the opportunity? Asking something as simple as, "Have you been to this event before?" or "I can't decide which flavor of jam to buy—do you have a favorite?" can open the door to a friendly conversation.

And here's the best part: if you don't exactly get the response you were hoping for? No biggie. In the world of old-school dating, rejection is just a part of the process—and it's not personal. Take a deep breath, smile, and move on. The world is full of opportunities, and the next person you meet could be your perfect match.

The Art of Flirting: Charm Without Technology

Let's be real: flirting is fun. And it's even more fun when you're not doing it over a text message or a screen. When you flirt in person, it's about energy, body language, and the little moments of connection that make your heart skip a beat. No need for emojis or GIFs here—just genuine connection.

Here are a few tips to keep your flirting game strong:

- **Body Language**: A relaxed posture, a little tilt of the head, and leaning in slightly when they're talking—all of these things show interest without you having to say a word. Just make sure it feels natural! If you're nervous, try taking a deep breath and focusing on being present.
- **Playful Banter**: Flirting is about playfulness, not pressure. A little teasing, a funny comment, or even sharing a personal anecdote can break the ice and help you both feel comfortable. And don't be afraid to laugh at yourself! Humor is an instant mood-lifter.
- **Be Curious**: Ask questions that show genuine interest in the other person. What do they like to do for fun? What's their favorite spot in town? People love talking about what excites them, so let them do the talking and follow up with thoughtful responses.
- **Compliments with Substance**: Instead of just saying, "You look nice," give them a compliment that's more specific: "That jacket really brings out the color in your eyes" or "You have a great laugh—totally contagious." It shows you're paying attention.

No Pressure: It's About Fun, Not Perfection
The beauty of old-school dating is that it's low pressure. You're not sending texts back and forth for weeks before meeting up—you're having a conversation, seeing where it goes, and deciding if there's potential. And let's face it: this whole dating thing should be fun, not stressful.

Whether you're meeting someone at a party, signing up for a dance class, or chatting in line at the bookstore, the key is to keep it light. Don't overthink it. Just enjoy the moment. And if there's chemistry? Great. If not? No problem! There are plenty of other people out there who are ready to meet you.

You've Got This—Confidence is Yours!
Look at you, all fired up and ready to take on the world of dating with confidence! Whether you've spent some time rebuilding or you're just starting to embrace your fabulous self, one thing is crystal clear: you're in a great place. You've worked on your mindset, rediscovered your strengths, and embraced who you are, flaws and all. That's more than half the battle right there.

Confidence isn't about being perfect—it's about being real. It's knowing that you've got something amazing to offer, and that whether or not a date goes as planned, you're still a catch. Life after 50 has so much to offer, and your confidence will continue to grow as you embrace the dating world with an open heart and a little bit of sparkle.

Remember, there's no rush. Confidence comes in layers, and each experience—each date, conversation, or new connection—only adds more depth. Take it one step at a time. Whether you're out there meeting new people, rediscovering old passions, or learning to love yourself all over again, you're on the right path.

Go ahead and step out there, hold your head high, and show the world exactly who you are. You've got everything it takes to make the most of this chapter. Dating after 50? You're not just ready for it—you're owning it! Let the adventure begin!

Chapter 3: Rebuilding Confidence—It's Your Time to Shine!

You might be looking for love or companionship, but what about that inner voice that says, *"Am I too old for this?"* or *"What if I'm not good enough?"* Trust me, you're not alone! Whether it's fear of rejection, insecurities about your appearance, or the worry that you'll never find someone who really "gets" you, all of these emotions are totally normal. But here's the good news—you've got everything you need to rebuild your confidence and feel fabulous in the dating world once again. Let's dive in and make sure you're stepping into the dating scene with a whole lot of sass, self-love, and strength.

Overcoming Fears and Insecurities: Letting Go of the Past

Let's face it: dating after 50 can bring up some old baggage. Maybe you've been burned by a past relationship, or you're scared of getting hurt again. Maybe you're worried about rejection, wondering if you still "got it." But the first step in rebuilding confidence is recognizing that your past doesn't define you—and that includes past heartaches, mistakes, and whatever baggage you're carrying around.

Let Go of Past Fears and Hurt

It's easy to get stuck in a cycle of "What if?" What if the person I meet isn't right for me? What if they reject me? What if I'm not as attractive as I used to be? The key here is releasing those fears. The truth is, nobody has the same experience as you, and while your past has shaped you, it doesn't have to hold you back from a bright future.

First things first: Start by giving yourself permission to move on. The best way to let go of the past is to forgive yourself for any mistakes you think you made. Let go of the "what ifs" and start focusing on the "what's next?" The fact that you're willing to date again shows just how strong you are. You've got this.

Building a Healthy Mindset Before Entering the Dating World

A healthy mindset is everything. Think of it as your emotional GPS—without it, you might get a little lost. Before you dive back into dating, take a moment to check in with yourself. What do you want? What are you ready for? What's important to you now that maybe wasn't before? Having clarity on what you want and need in a relationship will set the stage for success.

Here's how to start:
- **Be kind to yourself.** Every day is a new opportunity to embrace who you are, flaws and all.
- **Focus on the positives.** You've lived a lot of life, and every chapter has made you the wonderful person you are today. Celebrate your experience!
- **Stay open-minded.** The more open and flexible you are, the more opportunities you'll have to meet great people.

Rediscovering Your Unique Charms: Let's Talk About Why You're Irresistible

Okay, let's talk about what makes you YOU: the quirks, the wisdom, the laugh lines. At 50, you've probably seen it all, and that makes you one of the most fascinating, confident people around. It's time to step into the spotlight and show off your one-of-a-kind sparkle!

Celebrate Your Strengths and Imperfections

Here's a little secret: imperfections are sexy. Seriously. The things that make you "flawed" are often the very things that make you interesting, relatable, and lovable. Your quirks, your personality, your life experiences—they're what set you apart from everyone else out there.

Maybe you've got a quirky laugh, a unique hobby, or an offbeat sense of humor. Guess what? Those things make you authentic and irresistible. Don't hide them; own them! Be unapologetically YOU.

Why Experience is Sexy

You know what you want, you know what you don't want, and you're not afraid to speak your mind. That's incredibly attractive. Your life experience is your superpower. You've learned a lot, and that's something no one can take away from you.

Whether it's handling difficult situations with grace, knowing how to navigate conversation, or simply knowing how to take care of yourself, these little nuggets of wisdom make you more interesting and captivating than any 20-something could ever be.

How to Let Your Personality Shine

Here's a fun exercise: Think of three things that make you uniquely you. Maybe it's your love for adventure, your passion for cooking, or your ability to tell the best mom jokes in the room. Now, think about how you can let those things shine. Whether it's sharing a funny story on a date, trying something new, or simply showing up with confidence—let your personality speak for itself.

Building Confidence: Hobbies, Fitness, and Self-Care

Confidence isn't just about how you feel emotionally—it's also about how you feel physically and mentally. Taking care of yourself through hobbies, fitness, and self-care is the ultimate power move. When you feel good about yourself, it's like an energy boost that radiates outward, making you feel unstoppable.

Did you know that when you're doing what you love, you're glowing? Whether it's reading, painting, gardening, or cooking up a storm, engaging in activities that bring you joy fills your life with positivity. And guess what? That positivity shows. It gives you something to talk about on dates, it makes you more attractive, and it reminds you of just how amazing your life is.

Not only does it boost your confidence, but it's a great way to meet people who share your interests. Take up a class or join a group—you never know where it might lead!

Exercise and Self-Esteem: How Staying Active Can Boost Your Confidence

When you work out, you don't just tone your muscles— you tone your self-esteem. Exercise releases endorphins, those feel-good chemicals that improve your mood and make you feel more confident.

You don't have to train for a marathon (unless you want to!), but even a brisk walk, yoga, or dancing to your favorite tunes can help boost your mood and confidence. When you feel good in your body, you show up to dates and new experiences with an extra skip in your step.

How to Take Care of Your Mind and Body

Taking care of yourself isn't just about physical health—it's also about mental well-being. Practice mindfulness, meditate, or do things that help you feel centered and grounded. When you feel good in your mind, you're more likely to feel good in your body—and vice versa.

Start with small acts of self-care. Try a warm bubble bath, a nap, or even spending 20 minutes a day reading or journaling. It's about making yourself a priority and filling your cup before you can pour into others.

The Importance of Self-Love: The Foundation for Healthy Relationships

You've heard it before, but let me repeat it: Before you can truly love someone else, you've got to love yourself. I know, I know—it sounds a little cliché, but it's the truth. Self-love is the foundation of everything. Without it, you're not going to be able to attract or maintain a healthy relationship. When you love yourself, you teach others how to treat you. So let's get to work on that self-love!

Building a Healthy Relationship with Yourself

Treat yourself like your own best friend. That means giving yourself grace when you make a mistake, celebrating your wins (big or small), and speaking to yourself with kindness and respect.

Write yourself a love letter if you need to. Remind yourself of your strengths and how far you've come. Self-love isn't about being perfect—it's about accepting and appreciating who you are right now. Tuck that note/letter in a side table and re-visit it as necessary. What a great reminder of your awesomeness!

How to Practice Self-Compassion and Self-Respect
Be gentle with yourself. You've been through a lot, and it's okay to show yourself some compassion. Treat yourself with the same kindness and understanding you would show a close friend. When you mess up (because we all do), be patient and forgiving with yourself.

Self-respect is also a big part of this. Don't settle for less than you deserve. Set boundaries, communicate clearly, and don't be afraid to say "no" when something doesn't feel right.

The Link Between Self-Love and Attracting Healthy Relationships
When you truly love and respect yourself, you'll attract people who reflect that energy. Healthy self-love is magnetic. It radiates from you, and people will take notice. You won't just accept any relationship—you'll seek out the ones that match your standards. You get what you give. Your brightness will beam out of your like sunshine. Now that is attractive!!

Time to Shine
When it comes to rebuilding your confidence, there's no one-size-fits-all approach. It's all about embracing who you are, celebrating your strengths, and building yourself up through self-care and kindness. You've got everything you need to thrive—so go ahead and step into that dating world with confidence. Whether it's trying something new, laughing your way through an awkward date, or simply being unapologetically yourself, you're ready for this next

chapter. And who knows? Love could be waiting just around the corner.

Chapter 4: Getting Started with Online Dating

Alright, let's talk about the digital revolution that has taken over the dating world. Forget about those days when you had to rely on chance encounters at parties or in the grocery store (though, we're not totally giving up on those magical moments). Now, all you need is your phone, a cup of coffee, and a dash of curiosity to jump into the exciting world of online dating.

I know, I know. It sounds a little intimidating. But don't worry, I'm here to guide you through it.

The world of online dating might seem like a strange, new galaxy at first—filled with swipes, profiles, and messaging lingo—but it's really just a modern way to meet new people. And guess what? You've got this! If you can navigate social media, text your friends, and maybe even work your way around Google, then online dating is absolutely within your reach. Plus, it can be so much fun once you get the hang of it.

Step 1: Creating a Compelling Profile

Picture this: you're setting up your online dating profile, ready to put your best foot forward. But wait—what does that even mean? What do you say about yourself? How do you make it sound like you, without getting too carried away?

Authenticity is key. You don't need to pretend to be someone you're not. But you do want to put your best self out there in a way that reflects who you really are—and what you're looking for. Whether you're after a casual connection or something more serious, your profile is your chance to show off your personality, share a little about your life, and let people know what you're looking for.

Let's break it all down

Your Bio: This is your "elevator pitch," and it's your opportunity to show off your personality. Keep it light and fun, but also be honest. But what should you include?

- **A little about you**: What do you love to do in your free time? What's your passion? Whether it's cooking, hiking, reading, or volunteering, this is your chance to share something that's uniquely "you."
- **What you're looking for**: Are you looking for someone to go on adventures with? A coffee buddy who's up for a good conversation? Or maybe you're searching for a more serious relationship. Being clear about your intentions will help attract people who want the same thing.
- **Humor**: A little wit can go a long way. Humor is magnetic! Show your playful side in your bio—it'll help people feel like they already know you before you even say a word.

Your Photos: Ah, the photos! Yes, they matter—but don't overthink them. You don't need a professionally done photoshoot (unless you want to!) but you do want your photos to reflect who you are.

- **The profile photo**: This should be a picture of your face. Keep it natural—no sunglasses or hats that hide your smile. People want to see you as you are. And make sure they are current – remember those pesky little "fake" profiles? Avoid doing the switcha-roo where you look older in real life than the picture you used.

- **Action shots**: Show off your interests! Whether you're hiking, cooking, painting, or laughing with friends, this gives people a window into your life.
- **The no-filter rule**: Filters can be fun, but they're not the best way to show your true self. Authenticity is sexy, so skip the heavy editing and just be you!

Step 2: Messaging: How to Break the Ice (Without Sounding Like a Robot)

Now that your profile is all set up and looking fabulous, it's time to dive into the messaging game. The first message is always the trickiest, right? You don't want to come off too eager (but not too aloof either). It's all about finding that sweet spot between being confident and being conversational.

Always start with something personal. Look at their profile and find something you genuinely want to know more about. This shows that you're not just sending a generic "Hey, what's up?" to everyone, but that you've actually taken the time to read their profile and show some interest.

For example:
- "I saw you're into hiking! Do you have a favorite trail around here?"
- "You mentioned that you're a dog lover. What's your pup's name? I'm a sucker for cute dogs!"

Not only does this feel more natural, but it also invites the person to share something about themselves, making the conversation flow more easily.

Now, here's what NOT to do:

- **Don't be cheesy**: Lines like "Are you a magician? Because whenever I look at you, everyone else disappears" are funny in the movies, but in real life, they can come off as a bit much. Just be yourself.
- **Don't be too forward**: Give them space to respond to your opening message. You can be flirty, but don't dive in too quickly with "So, when can I take you out for dinner?" Let the conversation build naturally!

The key to great messaging? Timing. Don't overthink your responses, but also don't leave someone hanging for days. A little back and forth goes a long way toward building a connection.

Step 3: Warning Signs and Staying Safe Online

Now, I know online dating can be a lot of fun, but we've also got to talk about staying safe. There's no need to freak out, though—I promise you, you're more in control than you might think.

Here are a few things to watch out for:

- **Vagueness**: If someone's profile or messages seem too vague or they refuse to share anything about themselves, that's a red flag. Authentic people are willing to share details about their lives.
- **Moving too fast**: If someone pressures you for your phone number, email, or personal details too quickly, it's a red flag. You want to take your time

getting to know someone before diving into more personal territory.

- **Too good to be true**: If someone's profile picture looks like it belongs in a magazine (and they're saying all the right things), don't be afraid to ask questions. Trust your gut, and if something feels off, take a step back.

Now, the number one rule for online dating safety? Trust your instincts. If something feels fishy, don't be afraid to block or report a profile. You're in control of the conversation and the pace of your interactions.

Step 4: Taking the Plunge: First Date Nerves and Excitement

Congratulations! After a few days of chatting, you've decided to take the next step and meet in person. Yay! The first date is always a little nerve-wracking, but it's also so exciting.

Here's how to keep things light, fun, and relaxed on that first date:

- **Pick a neutral location**: If you're feeling a little nervous, meet in a public place like a coffee shop or a casual café. It's low-pressure, easy to talk, and you'll both feel comfortable in a neutral setting.
- **Stay true to yourself**: If you're nervous, don't try to be someone you're not. Just relax, smile, and enjoy the moment. Remember, this is about getting to know each other, not impressing anyone.
- **Don't overthink the details**: There's no need to plan every little moment. Let the conversation flow naturally. And if things aren't perfect? No big deal.

Not every date is going to be fireworks, and that's okay.

The key is to enjoy the journey. Whether it's a first date that leads to a second or just a fun evening of laughs and good conversation, online dating is about connection. Sometimes it takes a few tries to find the right match, but that's all part of the fun!

Step 5: Managing the Emotional Rollercoaster
Online dating isn't all sunshine and roses (though, when it's good, it's pretty close!). There will be highs, lows, and moments where you might question whether you're doing this right. But let me tell you something: you are.

Here's how to handle the emotional ups and downs:
- **Don't take things personally**: If someone doesn't respond, or if a date doesn't lead to another, it's not a reflection of you. Not every connection is meant to be. Keep your head up and keep going.
- **Enjoy the ride**: The fun of online dating is the journey, not just the destination. Meet new people, try new things, and enjoy the excitement of each connection—whether it turns into something lasting or just makes for a great story.

Time to Hit "Send"—You've Got This!
Well, look at you! You've crafted a killer profile, navigated the world of online messaging, and are officially ready to dive into the digital dating pool. Sure, it can feel a little intimidating at first, but guess what? You've totally got this. Dating after 50 in the online world is all about having fun, being authentic, and taking it one step at a time.

The great thing about online dating is that you can move at your own pace—there's no rush. You get to set the tone, steer the conversation, and decide who's a good match for you. Whether you're just dipping your toes in or diving headfirst into a few dates, remember that this is all part of the process. Each message, each profile, and each conversation brings you closer to finding someone who's truly a good fit.

And hey, don't forget to be kind to yourself through it all. You'll have your highs and lows, and that's totally normal. If you don't hit it off with someone, just chalk it up to experience and move on. The more you put yourself out there, the more you'll learn about what you really want (and what you don't). Online dating isn't a race—it's a journey. And guess what? You're in the driver's seat.

Go ahead, hit "send" and start chatting. Your next great adventure might just be a click away! Whether it's a lasting connection or just a fun conversation, you're making progress every step of the way. Dating after 50? It's not only possible—it's exciting, and you're absolutely ready for it!

Chapter 5: Navigating First Dates—Let the Fun Begin!

Look at you - you've done the hard part. You've swiped, you've chatted, and you've decided that yes, this person is worth meeting IRL. You're both excited, a little nervous, and maybe even a tad unsure of what exactly you're walking into. It's totally normal! First dates are like blindfolded dances—sometimes it's awkward, sometimes it's magical, and sometimes it's just about having a good laugh and not taking things too seriously.

But guess what? There's no need to panic. First dates after 50 can actually be way more fun than when you were younger. You know yourself better, you're more comfortable in your skin, and you're just a lot less likely to sweat the small stuff. Plus, you've got years of life experience to make those initial jitters feel like a walk in the park.

Here's your ultimate guide to acing that first date with style, charm, and a lot of laughs along the way.

Set the Stage with a Fun, Low-Key Location
We know, we know—the first date is nerve-wracking, and choosing the right spot can feel like picking the perfect outfit. But don't overthink it! You want a location that feels casual, comfortable, and allows for easy conversation. This is not the time for a fancy, quiet restaurant where the only sound is the hum of your nervous heartbeat. You're here to get to know each other, not to worry about what fork to use.

Here are some perfect first date spots that set the right vibe:

- **Coffee Shop**: You can't go wrong with a cozy, low-pressure coffee shop. It's a great place for chatting without the noise or distractions of a fancy dinner. Plus, if the date's going well, you can always linger over another cup of joe. If not? You've got an easy out.
- **Casual Café or Bistro**: A laid-back café with a variety of food options gives you something to nibble on without feeling like you're making a big commitment (both in terms of food and time). The key here is that you can still talk, laugh, and really get to know each other in a relaxed setting.
- **Local Brewery or Wine Bar**: Non-judgmental and fun! A local brewery or wine bar (without going overboard on the wine, of course!) offers a casual, fun atmosphere where you can both sample new drinks, chat about your favorites, and bond over shared tastes.
- **Outdoor Adventures**: If you're both into nature, an easy walk in the park, a hike, or a visit to a local botanical garden can be perfect for a first date. There's something about fresh air and nature that makes people feel relaxed and connected.
- **Art or History Museum**: A stroll through an art or history museum is a perfect way to bond over mutual interests and keep things light. Plus, having interesting things to discuss while strolling gives you so much to talk about.

Pro Tip: Whatever you choose, make sure it's a place where you can comfortably talk and connect. The goal is conversation—not just sitting in silence because the atmosphere is too loud or distracting!

Keep the Conversation Flowing (And Have Fun with It!)
Okay, so now you're at the date, and the conversation's the star of the show. We know, small talk can feel like the ultimate first-date villain, but it doesn't have to be! You've got the experience, the stories, and the charm to carry this off. Plus, you've already been chatting online, so there's a solid base to build on.

Here's the trick: ask open-ended questions. These are the questions that invite your date to share a bit more about themselves, rather than just giving a "yes" or "no" answer. Think: "Tell me about your favorite trip," instead of "Have you been on vacation recently?"

Here are some questions that will get the ball rolling (and keep it rolling!):
- "What's something on your bucket list that you'd love to do?"
- "Do you have any hobbies or activities that you're passionate about?"
- "What's the most memorable adventure you've been on?"
- "I'm always looking for new book recommendations. What's the best book you've read recently?"
- "What's something unexpected or surprising about you that most people wouldn't guess?"

These types of questions open up the conversation and give you a chance to learn more about each other without the pressure of feeling like you're on a job interview. If they mention something you're interested in, go with it! Be curious and ask follow-ups.

And hey, don't forget to laugh! A little humor goes a long way. Whether you share a funny travel story, talk about the most bizarre thing you've eaten, or reminisce about a time you've totally embarrassed yourself (we all have those stories!), laughter is a surefire way to break the ice and make the night memorable.

Relax, Be Yourself, and Embrace the Imperfections
The number one thing to remember on a first date? You don't have to be perfect. In fact, it's the imperfections that make things interesting. Let's be honest: nobody's expecting you to be flawless. If you drop your fork or spill a drink (hey, it happens!), laugh it off and move on. It's all part of the experience.

This is your chance to show up as your true self—quirks, flaws, and all. Embrace your uniqueness, whether it's the way you laugh or the fact that you're obsessed with crossword puzzles. People are attracted to authenticity, not perfection. Besides, if they like you for who you really are, that's a win!

Pro Tip: If you're nervous, that's okay! Just take a deep breath. There's no need to put on an act. Everyone gets nervous, and most people are far more relaxed than you think. If you feel awkward, laugh it off—chances are, they're feeling the same way!

Keep It Light, Keep It Fun, and Don't Overthink It
One of the best things about dating after 50 is that you've got a lifetime of experiences to pull from—and you know

how to have fun with it. On a first date, keep things lighthearted and playful. The goal is to enjoy getting to know someone new—not to figure out the future in one evening.

If the date's going well, fantastic! You can talk about future plans, maybe even get a little flirty. If it's not clicking, that's okay too! Not every date will lead to a love story, and that's perfectly fine. The important thing is that you're out there, putting yourself out there, and having fun along the way.

If you're enjoying yourself, maybe suggest a second date idea on the spot: "I know a great little jazz bar, how about we check it out next weekend?" This keeps the momentum going and shows that you're interested in seeing them again—but without the pressure of making it feel like a huge decision.

And if it's clear that it's not a match? That's cool, too. Thank them for the date, be polite, and don't feel like you have to force a connection. The dating world is about finding someone who clicks with you—and not every date will be that person.

The Follow-Up—Let's Keep This Going!
Okay, so the date is over, and it was either amazing or just... okay. No matter what, the follow-up is key. If you're interested in seeing them again, let them know. A quick text the next day saying, "Hey, I really enjoyed our time together—let's do it again sometime" is a perfect way to express your interest without coming on too strong.

If it wasn't quite the spark you were hoping for, that's fine, too. You can always be polite and kind, and let them know you didn't feel a connection. It doesn't have to be awkward—just be honest and respectful. Remember, dating is all about finding the right fit!

And That's a Wrap on First Dates—Now Go Have Fun!
Woohoo, you've survived the first date! Whether it was a complete hit, a little awkward, or a learning experience (hey, it happens), you've done something huge—you put yourself out there. And guess what? That's what dating's all about: showing up, being yourself, and seeing where the adventure takes you.

First dates after 50 are a total vibe. You've got the wisdom to roll with the punches, the confidence to laugh at yourself, and the life experience to know that not every date has to be "the one" to be worthwhile. Whether you're looking for a soulmate or just someone to share a laugh with, there's no pressure. It's all about having a good time and letting things unfold naturally.

So, what's next? If you had fun, awesome! Text them the next day with something light and flirty, and maybe suggest a second date. If it wasn't a match, no worries! You're out there meeting new people, having new experiences, and learning more about what you really want. Keep it light, keep it fun, and most importantly, keep going.

Remember that first dates are just the opening chapter in a much bigger story. So, get ready to write your own. Keep your heart open, your mind curious, and your sense of humor sharp. The world of dating after 50 is yours to explore—one fun, flirty date at a time. Let the next adventure begin!

Chapter 6: Dealing with Life Experience— Because You've Lived, Loved, and Learned!

Dating after 50 isn't just about finding someone to grab a bite with or catch a movie on a Friday night. Nope, it's about diving into a whole new world of *life experience*— and let's be honest, you've got a ton of that. You've been through relationships, ups, downs, family drama, and a whole bunch of wild adventures (or at least the ones you tell your friends about over margaritas). But how do you take all that *wisdom*—yes, we're calling it wisdom, not baggage—into your dating life without scaring someone off? Don't worry, I've got you covered. In this chapter, we're going to talk about how to embrace your past without letting it take over your future, and how to juggle your busy life with the pursuit of love.

Embracing Your Past Without Letting It Define Your Present

Let's face it: by the time you hit 50, you've probably racked up a hefty collection of love, loss, wins, and "oops" moments. But here's the golden nugget of wisdom: your past doesn't have to drag you down. Sure, it shaped who you are, but it's not the *entire* story. The secret to confidently dating after 50 is embracing all those experiences without letting them take center stage.

Celebrate Your Journey

Your life story is like a multi-season drama, full of plot twists, character development, and—let's be honest—a few cliffhangers. Whether you've been married, raised kids, built a career, or took a spontaneous year off to travel the world (you do you), those experiences are what make you *fascinating*. But here's the deal: dating at 50+ is about your next chapter, not a rerun of your greatest hits.

So, when you're getting back into the dating game, rock your life experience like a badge of honor—not a suitcase full of emotional baggage. It's not about past mistakes; it's about the wisdom you've gained. Who you were then doesn't have to dictate who you are now. So go ahead—let go of any guilt, regrets, or outdated narratives, and fully embrace the amazing person you've become. This is your time to be unapologetically you and enjoy what's next!

Talking About Kids, Exes, and Finances—Without Oversharing

Ah, the tricky topics: kids, exes, and money. Let's break it down so you can navigate these with ease, without sounding like you're auditioning for a reality show.

Talking About Kids

We know your kids are a big deal—whether they're living their best adult lives or still hanging around your house, raiding your fridge. But when it comes to dating, try to keep it light. Instead of a full rundown on your kid's latest drama, maybe share a funny anecdote or casually mention how they're doing. The goal is to let your kids be part of the conversation, not the *whole* conversation.

And if your date has kids too? Awesome. Find common ground, but remember: no one needs a competitive "my kid's the best" showdown. Keep it chill and let things flow naturally.

Talking About Exes
The *ex-factor*—ah yes. We all have a past. But remember, when you're dating someone new, they're looking to build something with *you*, not dive into your backstory. Keep the ex-talk brief and positive. A simple "I'm on good terms with my ex" or "I've learned a lot from my past relationships" will do the trick.

And as tempting as it might be to share the juicy details of why your last relationship ended, hold off. No need to unload all the drama—save it for a deeper connection down the road. Keep it light, keep it positive, and let the past stay where it belongs: behind you.

Talking About Finances
Money talk can be... awkward. While you definitely don't need to discuss bank balances over coffee, it's a good idea to be open about your financial situation once things get more serious. If you're heading toward a long-term relationship, understanding each other's financial goals will be key. But for now? Just don't pull out the credit report on date one.

Dating with Kids: Balancing Family Life and Romance

Dating with kids in the picture? Oh, it's a balancing act—but don't worry, you can totally juggle it. Whether your kids are grown, still living at home, or coming by for weekend visits, they're a huge part of your life—and they'll need to be considered as you dive into new relationships.

Setting Boundaries
You love your kids, but you deserve some "me" time too. Don't feel guilty for carving out space for romance. Make sure your date knows you're a loving parent, but you also need time to connect as a couple. Balance is key.

Introducing New Partners to Your Kids
Introducing a new partner to your kids? That's a big step. Take it slow—no need to rush things. If your kids are younger, be especially mindful of their feelings. Let the relationship grow naturally before making any big introductions. It's all about timing—and don't pressure anyone to form instant bonds.

Navigating Dating with Grandkids in the Picture
Ah, grandkids. If you're lucky enough to be a grandparent, you know they add a whole new layer to your life. They bring joy (and a little chaos) but also need time and attention. Finding time for both your grandkids and your date? It's doable, you just have to be mindful.

Grandkids as Your "Secret Weapon"

Grandkids are a perfect icebreaker! Everyone loves to talk about kids and grandkids, so casually drop a funny story or mention how adorable they are. But remember, don't let your grandkids take over the conversation. Let your partner know that while your grandkids are important, there's room for romance too.

Blended Families and Navigating Second Chances
So you've met someone special—and they've got kids (or maybe you do). Suddenly, you're in the world of blended families. Don't panic! Blended families are all about patience, communication, and *lots* of understanding. Second chances at love are a beautiful thing, and creating harmony can absolutely happen.

Communicate Openly
The key here is honest conversations. What kind of boundaries are you both comfortable with? What traditions are important to each of you? Discussing these things up front will save a lot of stress down the road.

Creating New Traditions
As you blend families, make sure to create new traditions that are unique to your relationship. Maybe it's a special weekend getaway, or a family dinner where everyone pitches in. It's about making new memories while honoring the ones your kids or grandkids already cherish.

Balancing Independence with Vulnerability
Here's the thing: you've spent years building your independence—whether it's through hobbies, career, or just getting really good at being on your own. But now you want to open up and be vulnerable to someone special. How do you find that balance?

Give Yourself Permission to Be Vulnerable

Independence is awesome, but vulnerability is what deepens connections. Trust me, it's one of the most attractive qualities you can bring to the table. So let yourself lean in, trust a little deeper, and be emotionally available—while still holding on to your sense of self.

Sharing Your Retirement Dreams: Aligning Future Goals

If retirement's on the horizon (or you've already crossed that bridge), you're probably thinking about what comes next. Do you and your partner want to travel? Start a business? Volunteer? It's time to get on the same page about your long-term goals.

Discuss Your Plans Early

Talking about retirement plans early on is key. Do you both want adventure, or are you craving a peaceful life in the countryside? There's no right or wrong, but knowing each other's visions will help you build a more fulfilling relationship.

Adjusting to Lifestyle Differences: From Hobbies to Living Arrangements

Let's be real: when you date later in life, you're probably going to have a few differences—like, maybe your partner's a night owl and you're an early bird. Maybe they love to read in silence, while you're all about podcasts. Whatever it is, it's all about compromise and respect.

Create Space for Each Other's Lives

The secret here? Balance. Support each other's hobbies without losing your own identity. Communicate openly about how you'll share time together and apart—and make sure both of you feel comfortable and respected.

Embrace the Adventure Ahead

And there we go! Now that we've navigated the ins and outs of dating after 50—life experiences, family dynamics, and the quirks that make you *you*—it's time to embrace the journey ahead.

You've lived a full life, and now you're not starting over—you're starting a new chapter, armed with wisdom, confidence, and a whole lot of zest. Whether you're diving into a new relationship, exploring solo adventures, or just enjoying the freedom to date on your terms, this is your time to shine.

Dating after 50 is all about writing your own rules. No more timelines or expectations—just you, your past, and the exciting unknown ahead. So go ahead—get out there, be your amazing self, and show the world just how much fun life after 50 can really be. You've got this.

Let the adventure begin!

Chapter 7: The Fun Side of Dating – Because Love Should Always Be a Little Bit Fun!

Let's be honest: dating after 50 doesn't have to be all serious conversations and "when are we getting married?" discussions. No, no, no. Dating at this stage in life should be about enjoying yourself, rediscovering the excitement of meeting new people, and yes, having some fun along the way. If you're still holding onto the belief that romance has to be intense and heavy, I'm here to tell you it's time to throw that out the window. Life's too short to take it too seriously, especially when it comes to love.

In this chapter, we're diving into the fun side of dating: from flirting (yes, you're never too old to flirt) to trying new activities together and rediscovering youthful energy. Romance is supposed to make you feel alive and excited— and there's no reason why it can't be just as thrilling now as it was when you were younger. Let's get into it!

Flirting for Fun and Connection: You've Still Got It

First things first: flirting isn't just for the young—it's for everyone! Whether you're at a coffee shop, chatting online, or out at a social event, flirting is the most fun, low-pressure way to see if there's a connection between you and someone else. And guess what? At 50+ you've probably mastered it—your wit, charm, and confidence are all part of the package deal.

What's the Secret to Flirting After 50?

It's all about lightheartedness. Flirting doesn't have to involve deep, intimate conversations right off the bat. It's about the playful back-and-forth that leaves both of you smiling.

Compliment their outfit or their laugh. Drop a fun little tease. A wink here, a subtle touch there. It's the little things that let someone know you're interested without making it all about the pressure of finding a soulmate.

And don't forget, flirting is also an amazing tool to build rapport and chemistry. It's fun, feels spontaneous, and brings an element of playfulness to the table. The goal? Connection and chemistry—not perfection.

Bonus Tip: If you're online dating, flirt in your messages! A cheeky comment or playful banter is a great way to break the ice and show you're not just looking for something serious right off the bat. Keeping it fun helps set the tone for a laid-back, enjoyable experience.

Embracing Spontaneity and Adventure: You're Not Too Old for an Impromptu Road Trip

One of the greatest gifts about dating later in life is that you've got no time to waste—so why not take full advantage of it? That means embracing spontaneity. Who says you can't decide on a whim to jump in the car and go on a road trip, take a random weekend getaway, or try something new together just because it sounds exciting?

The Magic of Spontaneity

Spontaneity doesn't mean jumping out of an airplane (though if you're into that, go for it!), but it does mean saying "yes" to new experiences when the opportunity presents itself. Instead of overthinking it, say yes to an impromptu wine tasting, a last-minute dinner date, or even exploring a part of your town you've never been to.

The thrill of an unplanned adventure can create a sense of excitement and novelty in the relationship, and that sense of "we're in this together" is the foundation for great memories.

Pro Tip: Be the person who says, "Let's do something crazy!" Whether it's a spontaneous dance party in the living room or hopping on a plane to somewhere new, making room for a little unpredictability can add a spark to the relationship. Just because you're more mature doesn't mean you can't still be spontaneous and wild!

Trying New Activities Together: Salsa Dancing, Cooking Classes, and More!

Gone are the days when a dinner and a movie were the only acceptable date options. Dating after 50 is the perfect time to reignite that sense of adventure and explore fun new activities. Trying new things together can be a great way to bond, laugh, and experience something exciting as a couple (or potential couple).

Salsa Dancing Anyone?

- You're never too old to learn how to move your body to a spicy rhythm, and salsa dancing is a fantastic option! It's active, it's fun, and it'll make you feel like you're stepping into a movie scene. Don't worry if you have two left feet—most dance classes for beginners are low-pressure, and you'll have a blast stumbling through the steps together.

Cooking Classes

- If dancing isn't your thing, why not try a cooking class? It's a perfect date activity that involves creativity, teamwork, and most importantly, food. Whether you're rolling sushi, mastering a soufflé, or baking fresh pasta, cooking classes give you the chance to bond over something tactile—and you get to eat your creation together at the end. Bonus points if you do it in your own kitchen later on and make it a fun, ongoing activity!

Adventure Sports (Just a Little!)

- And hey, if you're feeling really adventurous, try an activity like kayaking, zip-lining, or even trapeze classes (yep, those exist!). Sharing these adrenaline-pumping moments can create an amazing sense of connection—because let's face it, you'll probably both be laughing (or screaming) the entire time!

Sharing Laughter: The Glue of Any Great Relationship

Let's face it: life can be messy, unpredictable, and at times a little bit stressful. But in any great relationship, laughter is the glue that holds everything together. When you can laugh together—whether it's over a shared joke, a funny mishap, or just because one of you is totally awkward—you know you've got something special.

Laughter as an Icebreaker

The more you can laugh in the early stages of dating, the stronger the foundation for the relationship. Think about it: you're both learning each other's quirks, discovering shared humor, and enjoying the simple moments. Humor can break down walls, and it can also help you get through any bumps in the road later on. Plus, it's pretty dang fun.

Share a Laugh
You don't have to have the perfect pickup line, but a good sense of humor? That'll go a long way. If you can make each other laugh, you've got a great shot at building a solid connection. Bonus points if you're both the types to laugh at yourself when something embarrassing happens—those moments are the ones that create unforgettable memories.

Rediscovering Youthful Energy in Romance
Romance has no age limit. That fluttery feeling in your stomach when you see someone you're interested in? It's just as real at 50 as it is at 25. Rediscovering your youthful energy in romance is one of the most exciting parts of dating at this stage in life. You've got the confidence and life experience, but you can still let yourself feel the spark that comes with fresh infatuation.

The Secret? Embrace Playfulness
A lot of people think romance means big, grand gestures or candlelit dinners. While those can be wonderful, real romance is often found in the small, playful moments—those little, silly things that make your heart race. Playfully holding hands while strolling through a park, sharing inside jokes, or just enjoying the buzz of a new connection—that's where the magic lies.

When you let yourself tap into that youthful energy, you'll notice how much more fun you're having. You might even feel like you're falling in love again—for the first time in years. And isn't that exactly what makes life exciting?

Traveling Together: Planning Romantic Getaways

Now that you've rediscovered your playful side, what better way to spice up the romance than by planning a getaway? Traveling with someone you like—or even love—can deepen your connection and create unforgettable memories. It's a whole different kind of adventure, full of exploration, new experiences, and plenty of opportunities for bonding.

Planning a Romantic Getaway

It doesn't have to be a fancy, expensive trip (though those are lovely too!). A weekend getaway to a charming nearby town, a beach retreat, or even a cozy cabin in the woods can do wonders for your relationship. Traveling together gives you the chance to see each other outside of your normal routines, and sometimes that's when the real magic happens.

The Best Part? Shared Adventures

Think about how fun it will be to try new foods, discover hidden gems in a city, or watch the sunset on a beach with someone who's as excited about the journey as you are. And when things go wrong (because let's be real, travel can be a bit unpredictable), you'll laugh about it together, creating even more memories along the way.

Dating Is Your New Adventure—Enjoy Every Moment

At the end of the day, dating after 50 is as much about enjoying the journey as it is about finding the right person. It's about trying new things, sharing laughs, embracing the no-pressure approach, and above all, remembering that life is meant to be fun. So, whether you're out on a spontaneous adventure, laughing over dinner, or simply enjoying a quiet moment, make the most of it. The fun side of dating is what keeps things exciting, fresh, and full of possibilities.

Remember: You've earned this stage of life. The adventures, the memories, the giggles, and the joy that come with it are yours to enjoy. And who knows? Maybe along the way, you'll find that spark, that connection, and that love that makes all the fun even more worthwhile. Ready to go make some memories? The world is waiting!

Chapter 8: Overcoming Challenges – Turning Obstacles into Opportunities

Dating after 50 might seem like an exciting new chapter, but let's face it, there are some challenges that come with the territory. Whether it's handling rejection, managing a busy schedule, or navigating physical changes, we've all got a few hurdles to jump over. The good news? You've got this! With your wisdom, life experience, and all the lessons you've learned along the way, you're more than capable of turning any challenge into an opportunity for growth and self-discovery.

In this chapter, we'll dive into how to handle life's inevitable challenges with grace, strength, and a whole lot of sass. From coping with rejection to dealing with financial concerns, we'll explore how to maintain your confidence and continue to thrive as you step into the dating world. Ready to overcome those obstacles? Let's get started!

Handling Rejection and Moving Forward with Grace
Let's be honest: rejection stings. Whether it's someone not responding to your online message, a date that doesn't lead to a second one, or someone you've developed feelings for who's just not that into you, rejection is never easy. But here's the thing—rejection is not a reflection of your worth. It's just part of the dating process, and while it might hurt for a bit, it's also a valuable opportunity to practice resilience.

How to Move Forward with Grace:

- **Acknowledge Your Feelings:** It's okay to feel disappointed, frustrated, or even a little bit sad. Feel those emotions, but don't let them dictate your next steps. Give yourself permission to feel hurt, but don't let it define you.
- **Keep Perspective:** Remember, not everyone is your person, and that's okay! Not every match will be a perfect fit, and sometimes someone just isn't in the right place to be a part of your journey.
- **Self-Compassion:** Treat yourself with the same kindness you'd offer a friend. Don't beat yourself up. Rejection is a redirection—it's guiding you to someone who will be a better match, someone who values you for all the right reasons.

Remember: rejection is part of the dating game, and it's an opportunity for you to get back out there and find someone who truly appreciates you.

Managing Time and Priorities in a Busy Life

Okay, here's the reality: we're all busy. Whether you're juggling work, family, or a hundred other things, carving out time for dating can feel like a challenge. But here's the secret—you can absolutely manage it. You just have to get creative and prioritize your time, like you do with everything else that matters in your life.

Time-Management Tips for Dating:

- **Set Boundaries:** As much as you'd love to drop everything and go on a spontaneous date, it's important to set boundaries around your time. Be honest with your date about your schedule. Communication is key!

- **Work with Your Lifestyle:** If you're busy with family, work, or hobbies, look for ways to integrate dating into your existing routine. Could you grab coffee with someone before a work meeting? Or go on a walk in the park on a weekend afternoon? Get creative with your date ideas to fit your life.
- **Quality Over Quantity:** Don't feel like you need to date constantly to make it work. It's all about making the quality time you spend together count. Whether it's a quick lunch date or an evening in, find ways to make every moment meaningful.

Balancing dating with everything else you've got going on doesn't have to be overwhelming. It's all about prioritizing your happiness and setting realistic expectations.

Coping with Physical or Health-Related Limitations

As we age, our bodies go through changes. You may experience physical limitations that make dating a little more challenging, whether it's mobility issues, chronic pain, or just the natural signs of aging. Here's the thing: these changes don't diminish your worth or your ability to love and be loved.

How to Cope with Health-Related Challenges:
- **Be Open About It:** If you're dealing with health issues, it's important to be upfront and communicate with your potential partner. Being open about your limitations helps to set expectations and ensures that your partner is compassionate and understanding.
- **Adapt Your Dates:** Just because you're not as spry as you once were doesn't mean you can't still have fun. Look for date ideas that work with your current physical abilities—whether it's a cozy

movie night in, a scenic drive, or a low-key dinner date. The key is to find what works for you and embrace it.

- **Celebrate Your Resilience:** Your health challenges may be part of your story, but they don't define you. What matters is your resilience, your ability to adapt, and your willingness to enjoy life and love even when things get tough.

A little physical change doesn't mean your love life has to slow down. You are still beautiful, vibrant, and deserving of love, and anyone worth your time will see that.

Dealing with Social Stigmas and Judgment
Society sometimes has a way of putting us into neat little boxes, especially when it comes to age and relationships. If you've ever been judged for dating at your age, or felt that subtle eye-roll from others when they found out you're looking for love, it can be frustrating. But here's the kicker—society's opinion doesn't matter. The only thing that matters is what makes you happy.

How to Handle Social Stigma:
- **Own Your Story:** You've lived a rich, full life, and anyone who judges you for dating later in life is just showing their ignorance. Own your choices and feel empowered by them. If someone doesn't get it, that's on them—not you.
- **Surround Yourself with Support:** The people who matter—your friends, family, and like-minded people—will support you in your dating journey. Don't waste time on people who make you feel bad about your choices.

- **Laugh It Off:** If someone makes a snide comment about you being "too old to date" or "still looking for love," smile and walk away. You know your worth, and that's all that matters.

Remember, age is just a number. If you're looking for love and connection, don't let anyone's outdated views stop you. Your happiness is what counts.

Learning to Set Healthy Boundaries
Ah, boundaries. They're crucial in any relationship— whether it's a romantic one, a friendship, or even with family. Setting healthy boundaries is about knowing what you need, what you're comfortable with, and being firm but fair in your expectations.

How to Set Boundaries:
- **Know Your Dealbreakers:** Before diving into any relationship, get clear on your non-negotiables. These are the things you absolutely cannot compromise on, whether it's trust, respect, or shared values.
- **Respect Yourself and Others:** Boundaries aren't just about what you won't tolerate—they're about respecting yourself and others' needs too. Be clear in your communication, and don't be afraid to say "no" when something doesn't feel right.
- **Be Consistent:** Setting boundaries is great, but it's important to stick to them. Don't let someone talk you into doing something you're not comfortable with just to avoid conflict.

Remember, healthy boundaries build healthy relationships. They create respect, understanding, and a sense of safety, which are the foundations of any lasting partnership.

Overcoming Fear of Retirement-Related Changes
As you look toward the future, you may feel a sense of fear or uncertainty about retirement. Will it change your sense of self? Will it affect your relationships? The answer? Yes, retirement can change things—but it can also open new doors for growth, purpose, and connection.

How to Embrace Retirement with Confidence:
- **Find New Purpose Together:** Retirement doesn't mean the end—it can be a new beginning. Use this time to focus on **shared goals** with your partner. Explore new activities, take that dream vacation, or work on projects together. Retirement can be a time to rediscover passions and create new dreams.
- **Stay Active and Engaged:** Don't let retirement make you complacent. Find ways to stay engaged with the world and continue growing. Whether it's starting a new hobby, volunteering, or even part-time work, staying active keeps you mentally and physically sharp.
- **Communicate Your Fears:** If you're nervous about retirement-related changes affecting your relationship, talk about it openly. **Communication is key**, and talking through your concerns can help you both navigate this transition with confidence and mutual support.

Think of retirement as an opportunity to write a new chapter in your love story—one that's full of new adventures, shared experiences, and even deeper connection.

Rebuilding Trust After Past Heartbreaks
We've all been there. Heartbreak can leave scars that take time to heal. If you've been hurt in past relationships, it's natural to feel hesitant about trusting again. But here's the good news—you can rebuild trust. And when you do, it's often stronger and more resilient than before.

How to Rebuild Trust:
- **Take Your Time:** Don't rush into anything. Healing takes time, and so does rebuilding trust. Be patient with yourself, and don't feel pressured to "move on" before you're ready.
- **Be Open and Honest:** Communication is essential for rebuilding trust. Be clear about your needs, boundaries, and concerns with your partner, and encourage them to do the same.
- **Believe in New Possibilities:** Just because you've been hurt in the past doesn't mean you'll be hurt again. Don't let the past dictate your future. There's someone out there who will respect and honor your trust, and you deserve that.

Addressing Financial Concerns: Planning for Love and Retirement
Money matters in any relationship, especially when it comes to retirement. Whether you're a retiree or just beginning to think about it, it's important to have honest conversations about finances. And guess what? It's possible to plan for love and retirement at the same time.

How to Tackle Financial Conversations:

- **Be Transparent:** Openly discuss your financial situation with your partner, and make sure you're on the same page about goals, spending habits, and retirement plans.
- **Plan Together:** Retirement planning can be fun when you do it as a couple. **Create a joint vision** for your future—travel, hobbies, or even a new business venture—and make sure your financial plans align with that.
- **Don't Sweat the Small Stuff:** Financial worries can sometimes feel overwhelming, but don't let them cloud your romantic life. Focus on the things that truly matter—love, connection, and the future you're building together.

Dating after 50 might come with its challenges, but the good news is that you're more than equipped to handle them. From handling rejection with grace to navigating the complexities of retirement, every challenge is an opportunity to grow, learn, and deepen your understanding of yourself and what you truly want in a relationship. Keep your head high, your heart open, and remember: dating after 50 is just the beginning of something amazing. You've got this!

Chapter 9: Finding What You're Looking For – Defining Your Ideal Relationship

Ah, so now you've ventured out into the world of dating after 50—hello, new connections, exciting possibilities, and, of course, endless potential for fun. But here's the kicker: with all the freedom and excitement of meeting new people, it's easy to get lost in the whirlwind of options. So how do you figure out exactly what you're looking for?

That's where this chapter comes in! We're about to dive deep into how to clarify your relationship goals, identify deal-breakers and must-haves, and ensure that you're truly compatible with someone before jumping in headfirst. Spoiler alert: it's not just about finding someone—it's about finding the right someone who fits into the life you've worked so hard to build. So grab your favorite mug of deliciousness, settle in, and let's get to it!

Clarifying Your Goals: Companionship, Romance, or Marriage?

What's your why? Why are you dating? Are you looking for a fun, lighthearted romance? A long-term companion to share your life with? Or perhaps, after years of living solo, you're thinking about diving into something more committed, like marriage? Knowing your relationship goals from the start is essential to navigating your dating journey.

Defining Your Intentions:

- **Companionship:** Maybe you're at a point in your life where you're craving someone to share the day-to-day with, but not necessarily looking for anything too serious. Companionship might mean enjoying activities together—whether it's hiking, cooking, or just binge-watching Netflix—without the pressure of labels.

- **Romance:** Perhaps you're interested in exploring the fun side of dating, enjoying the thrill of meeting new people, and experiencing romance without the expectation of it turning into something permanent. That's totally okay, too! Sometimes romance is exactly what you need to feel alive and inspired.
- **Marriage:** Maybe you're thinking about the next chapter, where a deep emotional connection and long-term commitment are what you're after. If that's the case, you'll want to be intentional about finding someone whose life goals align with yours, including what marriage looks like in the 21st century.

Here's the important takeaway: be honest with yourself about your goals. If you know you're just looking for some companionship or a fun fling, it's not fair to lead someone on who might be seeking a more serious, long-term relationship. And vice versa! Being clear about your intentions makes everything easier—and much more enjoyable—down the road.

Knowing Your Deal-Breakers and Must-Haves

Let's talk boundaries—and not just the "I need space to binge-watch Netflix in peace" kind. We're talking about those non-negotiables in a relationship, the things that are absolute deal-breakers for you, as well as the things you absolutely cannot live without.

What Are Your Deal-Breakers?

- **Values Mismatch:** If you're a huge animal lover and your date thinks pets are overrated, that might not be a relationship that's going to go the distance. Or if you're passionate about fitness and they're not willing to even take a walk with you, that's a red flag.
- **Poor Communication:** If someone consistently shuts down or isn't willing to have open, honest conversations, it can be a huge barrier to long-term happiness.
- **Life Goals:** You don't have to have everything in common, but if you're looking to travel the world and they want to stay home, there might be a disconnect.

And What Are Your Must-Haves?

- **Chemistry:** You can't fake it. A strong physical and emotional connection is the foundation of any romantic relationship. That spark matters.
- **Shared Interests:** It's not about finding someone who likes exactly what you do, but it's essential that you have some common ground—whether it's a shared love for travel, hiking, or a Netflix series you're both obsessed with.
- **Respect and Kindness:** Simple, but incredibly important. A person who treats you with kindness and respect—who makes you feel valued—is worth their weight in gold.

Know what you can't live with and what you can't live without. This clarity will save you time, energy, and potential heartbreak in the long run.

Signs of Compatibility and Emotional Connection
At this stage of life, you're probably not looking for someone to just "fill the void." No, you're seeking a partner you can actually **connect with**—emotionally, mentally, and spiritually. So how do you spot someone who's truly compatible?

Signs of Compatibility:
- **Emotional Availability:** A partner who is open and willing to share their thoughts, feelings, and vulnerabilities will create a deeper bond. If they're closed off, it might be a sign they're not ready for a relationship—or that you're just not the right match.
- **Similar Communication Styles:** You don't need to agree on everything, but how you communicate (especially during conflict) matters. If you both approach disagreements with respect and understanding, it's a good sign of compatibility.
- **Shared Values and Interests:** This is huge! Do you both want the same things in life? Do you enjoy the same types of activities? While it's okay to have differences, it's important to have enough in common to build a solid foundation.

Emotional connection is the glue that holds everything together. If you're not feeling that pull, it might be time to reevaluate. But if you find someone who gets you—who you can talk to for hours without feeling exhausted—then you're onto something special!

The Value of Taking Things Slow

One of the beautiful things about dating after 50 is that there's **no rush**. You've lived a rich life, and now, you can afford to take your time. There's no pressure to move things along quickly, and in fact, taking things slow can work to your advantage.

Why Slow Dating Works:

- **Building a Stronger Foundation:** By taking time to truly get to know each other, you create a stronger foundation for the relationship. You can explore emotional, mental, and physical intimacy at a pace that feels right for both of you.
- **Avoiding Rushed Decisions:** When you slow down, you give yourself time to evaluate whether you're truly compatible—not just infatuated. That means fewer mistakes, less drama, and more meaningful connections.
- **Building Trust:** Trust isn't built overnight, especially when you've been hurt before. The longer you take to get to know someone, the stronger the trust will be when it develops.

Remember: there's no expiration date on love. You don't have to rush into anything you're not ready for, and the best relationships tend to grow naturally, over time.

Exploring Casual Dating Versus Serious Commitment

Okay, let's talk about two paths that are totally okay to take: casual dating and serious commitment. You might be in the mood for a no-pressure, fun, low-stakes fling—or maybe you're looking for something long-term. Both are valid choices, but it's crucial to know what you're looking for from the start.

Casual Dating:
- **Less Pressure:** Casual dating can be about having fun, exploring connections, and enjoying the company of someone without the expectation of long-term commitment.
- **Exploring Different People:** It allows you to meet a variety of people and explore different types of relationships without the obligation of settling down.
- **Emotional Freedom:** With casual dating, you have the freedom to be independent while still enjoying the company of others.

Serious Commitment:
- **Long-Term Partnership:** If you're seeking a deep emotional connection and planning a future with someone, serious commitment is where you'll want to focus your energy.
- **Building a Life Together:** Serious dating is about shared values, goals, and making decisions together that affect both of your futures.
- **Deeper Intimacy:** In a committed relationship, you'll experience a deeper level of trust, intimacy, and long-term compatibility.

Both options can be fulfilling—it's all about your personal goals and intentions. Just make sure you communicate your desires clearly with your date so you're on the same page.

Discussing Long-Term Plans: Living Arrangements, Health, and Family Dynamics

When you're dating after 50, it's important to have some **real conversations** about the future. As you begin to build a relationship, discussing long-term plans is key to making sure your goals align.

What to Talk About:
- **Living Arrangements:** Are you planning on living together? Do you have your own homes and are open to sharing one? If either of you has children living with you, it's worth discussing how that might impact your living situation.
- **Health Concerns:** As we age, health becomes an increasingly important topic. It's important to be upfront about any existing health concerns and talk about how you both plan to maintain good health as you grow older.
- **Family Dynamics:** If either of you has children or grandchildren, it's helpful to discuss how these family relationships will factor into your relationship, particularly as they may influence your living arrangements, vacations, or holidays.

These conversations can feel a bit daunting, but they are so important for long-term happiness. You'll both feel more secure and connected when you know you're aligned on these big-picture issues.

Embracing Compromise and Finding Balance in Relationships

Finally, we come to the art of **compromise**. In any relationship, it's essential to find balance—not just in the little things (like who's picking up the takeout), but in the bigger picture.

Finding the Middle Ground:
- **It's Not All About You (or Them):** Sometimes, compromise means learning to let go of your preferences and make space for your partner's needs and desires. It's about finding a balance between what **you** want and what **they** want—and being flexible along the way.
- **Pick Your Battles:** Not everything requires a compromise. Some things, like your core values or deal-breakers, should be non-negotiable. But for the little things? Practice the art of **letting go**.
- **Create Win-Win Scenarios:** Compromise doesn't mean sacrificing your happiness. It means finding solutions where both partners feel valued and supported.

In relationships, compromise is key, but it's important that both partners are equally committed to making it work.

So, whether you're looking for companionship, romance, or a lifelong partner, you've got the tools to find what you're really after. Be honest with yourself, communicate openly, and remember: the best relationships are built on understanding, compatibility, and a willingness to grow together. Happy dating!

Chapter 10: Embracing Singledom – Celebrating Your Independence and Personal Growth

Being single after 50 is awesome! No, really—don't just take our word for it. Sure, the dating world can be a fun adventure, but there's also something incredibly empowering about embracing your own company. There's freedom, growth, and joy in being single—whether you're coming out of a long relationship, recovering from heartbreak, or simply enjoying the single life. Singledom isn't just a status; it's an opportunity to fully embrace yourself and your life, without needing validation from anyone else.

Let's dive in and explore just how fulfilling life can be when you're living for yourself, not for someone else. It's time to break free of the notion that being single is "lonely" or "missing something." Nope! Being single is a celebration of who you are, where you've been, and where you're going.

Celebrating Your Independence and Personal Growth

First, let's talk about independence—the freedom to live life on your terms, without having to consider someone else's opinions, needs, or schedule. Being single isn't a waiting room for your next relationship; it's a chance to thrive on your own.

Why Independence is a Superpower:
- **Your Time, Your Rules:** You get to spend your evenings however you like. Movie night in? Check. Staying out late with friends? Absolutely. You're

the boss of your calendar, and that's pretty darn exciting.

- **Personal Growth:** Without the distractions of a relationship, you have more time to focus on yourself—your hobbies, your career, your health. The sky's the limit when you're not compromising your dreams for anyone else.
- **No Negotiating:** Want to spend the weekend exploring a new hobby or catching up on your favorite series? No need to check in with anyone! You're free to do what you want when you want—and that's something to celebrate.

Being single is an opportunity for self-discovery and personal growth. You get to take a deep dive into what makes you tick, what you love, and where you're headed next. It's not selfish to spend time focusing on your own happiness—it's necessary.

Why Being Single Can Be a Fulfilling Choice
You know that old saying, "You complete me"? Well, here's the truth: you're already complete. The idea that you need a romantic partner to be fulfilled is a myth. In fact, embracing single life can open up a world of personal satisfaction and self-empowerment.

Why Singledom Rocks:
- **Self-Sufficiency:** There's something incredibly satisfying about handling life's ups and downs on your own. From paying bills to fixing a leaky faucet, you're the one making things happen. You are capable, resourceful, and, most importantly, independent.

- **No Compromise Necessary:** Single life means you get to call the shots. Want to travel solo? Go for it! Feel like redecorating the living room for the 10th time this year? Knock yourself out! Being single means you don't have to compromise your decisions or lifestyle for anyone else.
- **Personal Fulfillment:** When you're single, you can focus entirely on things that bring you **joy**—whether that's a new fitness routine, learning a new skill, or diving into your favorite hobby. The pursuit of your passions becomes your top priority, and that's incredibly fulfilling.

Being single doesn't mean you're lacking something; it means you're whole and capable of creating a fulfilling, vibrant life on your own.

Building a Rich Social Life Beyond Dating
Okay, let's be real—dating can be exciting, but it's just one part of a much bigger social picture. When you're single, there's an entire world of friendships and social activities waiting for you. And guess what? You don't need a romantic partner to have a full and rich social life.

Socializing Beyond the Date Scene:
- **Reconnecting with Old Friends:** After 50, it's easy to let friendships slip to the background as life gets busy. But being single gives you the perfect opportunity to **rekindle old friendships**—whether that's through coffee dates, phone calls, or impromptu weekend trips.
- **Making New Connections:** Without the pressure of finding a "romantic partner," you can focus on deepening **platonic relationships**. Join a local club,

take a cooking class, or sign up for a weekend retreat. You'll meet like-minded people who could become lifelong friends.

- **Strengthening Family Bonds:** Singledom is also a great time to strengthen your relationships with family. Whether it's spending more time with your kids, grandchildren, or siblings, the beauty of being single is that you have the flexibility to invest in your family without the distractions of a partner's schedule.

Building a rich social life is key to a fulfilling single life. The more you fill your calendar with meaningful connections, the less you'll feel like you're "missing" anything. Your friendships, family ties, and social circles will bring you all the joy and fulfillment you need.

Finding Joy in Self-Love and Solo Adventures
Let's talk about solo adventures. The idea of traveling alone or pursuing hobbies on your own can be intimidating at first, but it's one of the most empowering and joyful experiences you can have. When you're single, you don't need anyone else's approval or permission to explore the world or dive into new experiences.

Self-Love Adventures:
- **Traveling Solo:** Whether it's a weekend getaway to a new city or a month-long trek across the globe, solo travel is one of the most freeing experiences. You get to make all the decisions—where you go, what you do, when you do it. And it's all for you.
- **Taking Up New Hobbies:** Ever wanted to learn how to paint? Or take up dancing? When you're single, there's no one to hold you back from trying new

things. This is your time to be selfish—embrace that freedom and discover new passions.

- **Finding Peace in Solitude:** Solo adventures don't always have to be extravagant. Sometimes the best moments come from spending a quiet afternoon in a café with a good book, or taking a long walk through your favorite park. It's about finding joy in your own company.

Self-love is the foundation for everything. By prioritizing your own happiness and indulging in solo activities that nourish your soul, you'll learn to love and appreciate your own company more than ever.

Maintaining Friendships and Family Bonds as a Cornerstone of Happiness
When you're in a relationship, it's easy to become so focused on that connection that you neglect your friendships and family bonds. But when you're single, you have the opportunity to nurture the relationships that matter most.

Why Friendships and Family Are Vital:

- **Your Support System:** Friends and family are your emotional safety net. They're the people who've got your back no matter what, and they're often the ones who keep you grounded during tough times.
- **Quality Time:** Being single means you have more time to spend with people you genuinely care about. Whether it's hosting a dinner party, planning a family trip, or just hanging out on a Sunday afternoon, those moments of connection are priceless.

- **Shared Joy:** There's nothing quite like sharing laughter, milestones, and inside jokes with the people who truly know you. Whether it's your lifelong best friend or your daughter's kids, these relationships enrich your life in ways that nothing else can.

Singledom gives you the space to build a stronger support system. The more you invest in these connections, the more fulfilling your life will be.

Planning for the Future: Single Living and Personal Goals
Now that we've covered how amazing life can be as a single person, it's time to talk about planning for the future. Just because you're living solo doesn't mean you shouldn't have clear goals and a vision for the next chapter of your life.

What the Future Looks Like for You:
- **Retirement Planning:** If you're thinking about retirement, take some time to explore what that looks like for you. Whether it's downsizing your home, traveling more, or starting a new hobby, the future is your canvas. And as a single person, you can design it any way you like.
- **Personal Goals:** What do you want to accomplish in the next 5, 10, or 20 years? Whether it's learning a new language, running a marathon, or writing a book, setting personal goals will keep you motivated and inspired.
- **Financial Independence:** Being single also means you have full control over your finances. Take the time to set a financial plan for the future that aligns with your goals. Whether it's saving for travel, a

second home, or retirement, planning ahead ensures your future is as fulfilling as your present.

The beauty of being single is that you get to create the life you want, without needing to compromise. Take this time to dream big, set goals, and invest in your future happiness.

Living the single life after 50 is about embracing freedom, independence, and the opportunity to focus on your own growth. Being single isn't a void—it's a space for you to truly thrive. Whether you're enjoying solo adventures, nurturing deep friendships, or planning your future, this chapter of your life is full of possibility. So go ahead— celebrate your independence, embrace the journey, and most importantly, have fun doing it!

Conclusion: Your Journey Awaits

You Made It!! We're at the end of our little adventure through the exciting world of dating after 50. But don't worry, this isn't a "goodbye" moment; it's just the beginning. Your journey awaits. Whether you're about to step out on your first date after a long hiatus, rekindling your spark with a past flame, or simply taking a breather while you explore what's next, know this: dating after 50 is full of possibilities, and you're just getting started.

Let's take a quick moment to reflect on what we've learned together. And, more importantly, let's get ready to embrace the fun, the challenges, and all the unexpected joys that lie ahead.

A Recap of Key Lessons and Encouragement to Take the Leap

Dating after 50 can feel like a whole new ballgame, but you're more than equipped to play. We've covered a lot of ground, from rebuilding confidence and navigating online dating to embracing your past and moving forward with grace.

- **Confidence is Key**: Remember, the most magnetic thing you can wear is a smile and a dose of self-love. You're not just a collection of past experiences—you're a beautiful, confident person with a world of potential for new connections and adventures.
- **Enjoy the Ride**: Dating isn't a race, it's a journey. Whether you're out on a first date or taking time to get to know yourself better, every moment is a chance to learn something new. You're not looking

for perfection; you're looking for someone (or something) that aligns with who you are now.

- **Stay Open**: If there's one thing we've learned, it's to embrace the unexpected. Sometimes love comes when you least expect it—and sometimes, it's better than you ever imagined.

So, if you're feeling a little nervous about stepping out there, know this: you've got this. Whether you're looking for companionship, romance, or something deeper, you're in a position to get what you want—on your own terms. It's your time to explore, rediscover joy, and connect with people who truly resonate with you.

Now, if there's any part of you that's hesitating, let's gently remind you that there's no right or wrong timeline for love. Your journey is uniquely yours—and it's filled with as much joy, adventure, and connection as you decide to create.

Reminders to Have Fun, Stay Curious, and Embrace the Unexpected

While the world of dating has certainly evolved, there's one thing that's always remained true: dating should be fun. And we don't just mean that first date excitement—though that's definitely a highlight! We mean the whole process. Dating is an opportunity to meet new people, try new things, and embrace whatever comes your way with an open heart.

Here are a few fun reminders as you embark on your journey:

- **Stay Curious**: Each date is an opportunity to explore, learn, and grow. Be curious not just about the person sitting across from you, but about yourself too. What do you love now? What have you learned about yourself since your last relationship? Stay open to discovering new things about your needs, desires, and even your deal-breakers.

- **Embrace the Unexpected**: Love doesn't always show up in the way we expect. That person you least thought you'd click with could turn out to be your perfect match. Or maybe, the best part of your dating journey will be about learning more about who you are, what you really want, and how to embrace the beauty of the unknown.
- **Have Fun**: Yes, dating is about finding connection, but it's also about enjoying life and having new experiences. Take a cooking class, join a book club, or go salsa dancing—whatever makes you happy! Remember, the process is just as important as the outcome. And if you meet someone amazing along the way? Well, even better.

A Heartfelt Invitation to Share Your Own Story of Dating After 50

What has dating after 50 looked like for you so far? Maybe you've had some wild adventures (hello, online dating!) or maybe you've learned some valuable lessons along the way. Maybe you're just dipping your toes into the waters of dating again, or maybe you've been happily single and enjoying every moment. Whatever your story is, it's worth sharing.

- **What have been your biggest challenges?**
- **What surprising moments have made you laugh?**
- **How have your views on love and relationships evolved?**

Sharing your experiences not only helps others, but it also helps you process, celebrate, and reflect on your own journey. So, take a moment to think about your own dating story. Whether you write it down in a journal, share it with a friend, or send it out into the world, your experiences are important—and they're part of the bigger picture of what it means to date after 50.

Final Thoughts on Love, Life, and Connection
As we wrap things up, it's time for one last, big reminder: Love and connection are lifelong journeys. There is no "one way" to do this dating thing, and no matter where you are on your path, you are exactly where you need to be.

- Love isn't something you "find" like a treasure chest at the end of a map. Love is something you create—through your actions, your openness, and your willingness to keep showing up for yourself and others.
- The best relationships aren't based on perfection. They're based on understanding, compromise, and a shared desire to grow together. At any stage of life, a strong, fulfilling relationship can bring immense joy—and when you approach it with curiosity, patience, and a sprinkle of fun, the possibilities are endless.
- But don't forget that singleness is just as valid a path as being in a relationship. You are complete, whole, and full of love and potential, no matter your relationship status. Embrace your independence, cherish your friendships, and never underestimate the power of self-love.

Ultimately, love, life, and connection are about growth—growing with others, yes, but also growing with yourself. Embrace the journey ahead. Be open, be patient, be playful, and most importantly—be you. Whether you're navigating first dates or enjoying the joy of being single, this is YOUR time to shine.

Take a deep breath, trust the process, and go out there and live your best life. The world is full of surprises, and your next great chapter is just waiting to be written. Here's to the adventure—may it be filled with joy, love, and plenty of laughter.

Bonus Material

We've covered a lot of ground, but it's not the end yet! In this bonus section, I've included some fun and helpful extras to keep you inspired, safe, and prepared as you embark on your dating journey. Whether you're looking for creative date ideas, books to fuel your self-growth, or a few podcasts to inspire your heart, this section has you covered.

Quick Tips for Staying Safe While Dating

As exciting as it is to explore new relationships, *safety should always come first*. Whether you're dating online or meeting in person, a few simple precautions can ensure that your experience is fun, secure, and stress-free. Here are some quick tips to keep in mind:

- **Meet in Public Places**: For your first few dates, always meet in public. Cafes, restaurants, parks, and places with lots of people are ideal.
- **Let Someone Know Where You're Going**: Share your plans with a friend or family member. Text them your location and who you're meeting, so someone knows what's going on.
- **Trust Your Instincts**: If something feels off during a date, don't hesitate to leave. Your intuition is your best guide in situations where you feel uncomfortable or unsafe.
- **Don't Share Personal Information Too Soon**: Keep your personal details (like home address, financial information, and workplace) to yourself in the beginning stages of dating. Let trust and familiarity build before getting too personal.
- **Use Safe Dating Apps**: Choose dating apps with safety features (like photo verification and

messaging systems) and read reviews. Stick to trusted platforms that have safeguards in place.
- **Set Boundaries**: Be clear about what you're comfortable with and respectful of your date's boundaries too. Healthy communication is key! It is ALWAYS okay, to say No.

By following these simple tips, you can navigate the dating world confidently, knowing that you've taken steps to protect your personal safety and well-being.

Fun Date Ideas for Different Personality Types

Not every date has to be the same, and the best way to connect with someone is to find out what makes them tick. Here are some fun date ideas tailored to different personality types.

The Adventurer
- **Go for a Hike**: If you both love the outdoors, a scenic hike can be a great way to bond over shared experiences and enjoy some fresh air.
- **Explore a New Town**: Take a day trip to a nearby town or city neither of you have explored. Wander through charming streets, visit local attractions, and grab a bite to eat at a quirky café.
- **Amusement Park Fun**: For those who love a bit of thrill and nostalgia, an amusement park date is a playful way to enjoy each other's company.

The Creative Soul
- **Take a Pottery Class Together**: Get your hands dirty and your creative juices flowing with a pottery or art class. You'll bond over making something unique and have a great conversation while you're at it.
- **Attend a Local Art Gallery**: If you both appreciate culture, a visit to a local gallery or museum is a

wonderful way to explore art and spark interesting conversations.

- **DIY Craft Night**: If you're into crafting, plan a date where you both make something. Whether it's knitting, painting, or making your own candles, creating something together is a meaningful experience.

The Foodie

- **Farmers' Market Date**: Stroll through a local farmers' market, pick out some fresh ingredients, and then cook a meal together at home.
- **Cooking Class**: Join a local cooking class and learn how to make something new. You'll both be able to impress each other with your culinary skills afterward!
- **Food Truck Hop**: Take a little culinary adventure by checking out various food trucks in your area. It's a casual and fun way to sample different cuisines without committing to one restaurant.

The Homebody

- **Movie Marathon**: Pick a movie genre or series you both love and have a cozy movie night in. Don't forget the popcorn!
- **Board Game Night**: If you're into games, a low-pressure date like board games or card games can spark lots of laughter and friendly competition.
- **Cook Dinner Together**: Skip the fancy restaurant and have a laid-back evening cooking a meal together. The process of preparing food can be just as fun as the meal itself.

The Extrovert

- **Dance Night**: Whether it's salsa, swing, or just a night of karaoke, dancing is a perfect way to unleash energy and have fun together.

- **Live Music Concert**: If you both enjoy live performances, attend a concert or a local music venue. Music is a great way to connect and bond.
- **Trivia Night at a Pub**: If you're looking for a little competition with a side of fun, a trivia night at a pub is a great way to get to know each other while working as a team.

Recommended Reading and Resources for Personal Growth and Romance

Want to dive deeper into personal growth or romance? Here's a list of books, podcasts, and resources that will inspire you to keep learning, evolving, and connecting with yourself and others.

Books for Personal Growth and Self-Discovery
- **"The Gifts of Imperfection" by Brené Brown**: This book is all about embracing vulnerability and living authentically. A must-read if you're looking to build self-love and confidence.
- **"Daring Greatly" by Brené Brown**: Another one by Brené Brown, this book focuses on embracing courage, vulnerability, and connection—perfect for anyone navigating new relationships.
- **"The Power of Now" by Eckhart Tolle**: A guide to mindfulness, this book helps you stay present in the moment, which is crucial for embracing life and love after 50.

Books on Romance and Relationships
- **"Modern Romance" by Aziz Ansari**: A fun, humorous, and insightful look at dating in the digital age. Perfect for getting a more modern perspective on how relationships form.

- **"The Five Love Languages" by Gary Chapman**: Discover how you and your partner express love differently, and how to use that to deepen your connection.
- **"Men Are from Mars, Women Are from Venus" by John Gray**: A classic relationship book that helps you understand the fundamental differences between men and women in relationships.

Podcasts and Resources
- **The Love, Happiness, and Success Podcast**: This podcast covers everything from relationships to personal development, offering practical advice for navigating love at any stage.
- **Modern Love (NY Times Podcast)**: Real stories about love, relationships, and loss that will inspire, move, and resonate with you.
- **The Single Woman's Podcast**: This show is designed to empower and inspire single women, with discussions on navigating life and relationships.

Journaling Prompts for Self-Reflection and Goal-Setting
Journaling is a powerful tool for self-reflection and growth. Use these prompts to guide your thoughts and set meaningful intentions as you move forward on your journey:
- What are the three things I most love about myself right now?
- What do I want out of my next relationship? What qualities am I looking for in a partner?
- How do I want to feel every day, and what steps can I take to feel that way?

- What does "love" mean to me now compared to when I was younger?
- What fears or doubts do I need to let go of in order to embrace new love and experiences?
- What are my personal goals for the next year, and how can I use dating to help me grow?

A Checklist for Preparing Yourself to Re-enter the Dating World

Ready to get back out there? Here's a checklist to help you prepare mentally, emotionally, and physically for the exciting adventure of dating after 50:

- **Reflect on past relationships**: What did I learn from them? What do I want to do differently this time?
- **Embrace self-love**: Have I taken time to care for myself—physically, emotionally, and spiritually?
- **Clarify my relationship goals**: Am I looking for a casual connection, a committed relationship, or just a bit of fun?
- **Update my online dating profile**: Have I selected photos that show my true self? Does my bio reflect who I am today?
- **Set healthy boundaries**: Am I ready to clearly communicate my needs and desires while respecting others'?
- **Stay open to new experiences**: Am I ready to try new things, meet new people, and embrace the unexpected?

By walking through these steps, you'll be mentally and emotionally ready to jump into the dating world—whether online or offline—and create the future you desire.

That's it, my Awesomes! Go forth and enjoy this exciting chapter of your life. Love, fun, and adventure are waiting for you!

Made in the USA
Las Vegas, NV
06 February 2025

17637429R00049